There Is a God!

JEREMY P. TARCHER/PENGUIN
a member of Penguin Group (USA)
New York

There *Is* a God!

1,001

HEARTWARMING (AND HILARIOUS)

REASONS TO BELIEVE

Richard Smith *and*
Maureen McElheron

JEREMY P. TARCHER/PENGUIN
Published by the Penguin Group
Penguin Group (USA) LLC, 375 Hudson Street,
New York, New York 10014

USA · Canada · UK · Ireland · Australia
New Zealand · India · South Africa · China

penguin.com
A Penguin Random House Company

ISBN 978-0-399-16780-5

Printed in the United States of America
1   3   5   7   9   10   8   6   4   2

BOOK DESIGN BY EMILY S. HERRICK

There Is a God!

Introduction

....

Are you a doubter? A believer? Or just confused?
Not to worry because . . .

"There is a God." In a cold and lonely universe, how
often do we utter this phrase at life's true miracles?
Feeling your heart swell as you watch your little girl
struggle with an ice cream cone that's bigger than
she is. The blessing of a loving spouse. You had the
courage to say no to an aggressive telemarketer and
a controlling mother on the same day. And is it not
wondrous that customs merely smiled at the cheese,
wine, sausage, bread, corkscrew, knife and several
hotel towels in your carry-on?

There Is a God is a humble (but meticulously researched) compilation of the many things that make life wonderful and hopeful. Coming home to the sound of little feet running and hearing "Daddy!" Those suspicious little teeth marks on the cookies left out for Santa. Leaving the restaurant on a freezing night and discovering coat check gave you a warmer coat. And is it not marvelous that at seventy, you still ski with your original hips?

We hope you will think of these pages as little security blankets, gentle reminders of an entity, a Divine Presence, if you will, who soothes, watches over us, gives us hope and reassures us when things are not entirely bright.

1.

The Big Dipper

2.

The selfless missionaries
who volunteer to give your
dog a bath

3. A dry basement after the storm

4. A gallery event with palatable wine

5. "It's benign."

6. You're not the couple arguing at the table next to you.

7. You were wise enough to purchase travel insurance that covers disappointment.

8. Your cat, sitting motionless, listening to classical music

9.

Dolphins

10. The man your mother warned you about turns out to be great.

11. A hospital room with an ocean view

12. It's December 10 and you're done with your Christmas shopping (almost).

13. The famished shark nibbled your flippers and swam away.

14. Sincere air kisses from someone with great breath

15. No one laughed when you got up to tango.

16.

You thought twice before
hitting "Send."

17.

Those suspicious little teeth
marks on the cookies left
out for Santa

18.

The seashell you pick up on
the beach and hold to your
ear has iTunes.

Miracle #1:
....

Researchers are now suggesting that bacon reduces one's risk of cardiovascular disease.

19.

Friends who help you
move for a six-pack

20.

You have all the ingredients for a relaxing night at home: a loaf of bread, a jug of wine and your iPhone.

21. The cute girl at the party came without a date.

22. Feeling your heart swell as you watch your little girl struggle with an ice cream cone that's bigger than she is

23. Your daughter finally fell for a nice guy.

24. You outsourced the worst of your teen years.

25. Results will not vary.

26. Your dentist would kill for your gums.

27. You and Oprah share a trainer.

28. A woman president

29. A paid internship

30.

Getting back your stolen
wallet with an apology and
an extra fifty dollars inside

31. You have no idea what "push-back" means.

32. In vino *veritas* (especially an extraordinary vintage)

33. Your temper at work is a protected disability.

34. A sticky love ballad just when you need one

35. Your four-year-old's impression of you when you're angry

36. The shoulder you're crying on belongs to a really buff body.

Miracle #2:

You managed to keep a lid on your weight during the holidays.

37.

Your hubby looks even
hotter when he pushes
a stroller.

38. Good-night hugs from your little girl

39. Going food shopping while hungry and spending only $369.44. (Last time this happened, you spent $512.77.)

40. The speeding cab splashed the guy in front of you.

41. Running into an old flame at the finish line of the marathon with your makeup still intact

42. You won the lawsuit against Sara Lee for forcing you to gain fifty-eight pounds.

43. You're smart enough to follow the advice of your fortune cookie ("Add the check carefully").

44.

You have the one mother in
the Western Hemisphere
who didn't throw out her
son's baseball cards.

Miracle #3:

....

Your first hole in one

> ## Miracle #4:
>
> ....
>
> Watching your toddler take his first wobbly steps

45. You never hear the people above you.

46. Blessed are the meek, for they don't object when your stuff takes up the entire overhead bin.

47. You easily name all Seven Dwarfs when the trooper administers the sobriety test.

48.

Fireflies on a June night

49. A second chance

50. You go your own way (even when Yelp says not to).

51. Your good health

52. You still think arthritis is a star in a distant galaxy.

53. Minimum payment due: $0.00

54. An airtight alibi

55. You always land on your feet.

56. A loony but loving aunt who helps you blossom socially

57. The campground where you've pitched your tent is near a Hilton (just in case).

58. He knows what a sham is.

59. And a dust ruffle.

60. He's not sure what a peplum is.

61. Summer love

62. The romance of doing laundry together

63. The app that separates whites from colors

64. You're even wittier when you're loaded.

65. The surprise drug test is multiple choice.

66. The statement "Just set it and forget it" perfectly describes your husband in a La-Z-Boy.

Miracle #5:

Time travel lets you go back and change your SAT scores.

67. You run into Woody Allen at a cocktail party and your joke about Stalin's gym shorts cracks him up.

68. The divorce doubled your closet space.

69. It's a poppy seed, not a bedbug: Poppy seed · Bedbug 🪰. (Note difference.)

70. You've been awarded a Medal of Freedom for your barbecued ribs.

71. You're the life of the quilting bee.

72. The shop managed to get the McNugget grease out of the seat of your Lamborghini.

73. Those free samples of men from Match.com

74. He left quietly while you feigned being asleep.

75. Everybody isn't having more sex than you.

76. The earth really did move.

77. A scented Valentine e-mail from your husband

78. Love at first sight, that endures

79. He didn't feel threatened when you asked for a key.

80. The club car

81. The tapas at that little place in Barcelona

82. *Singin' in the Rain* gets better each time you see it.

83. A morning-after pill that alleviates serious hangovers

84. Your stream-of-consciousness admissions essay got you into MIT.

85. And a Rhodes Scholarship.

> ### Miracle #6:
> ....
>
> He remembered to put the toilet seat back down.

86. Listening to a sleeping baby's soft, gentle breathing

87. The complimentary chocolate on your hotel bed is the same size as the pillow.

88. According to the body mass index (BMI) chart, you're too short for your weight.

89.

The mariachi band totally
missed your table.

90.

She thinks you look elegant
in a Hawaiian shirt.

91. Instead of giving you general anesthesia, they let you stroke your cat.

92. The wonder of Intelligent Design (your awesome new yoga butt)

93. Your arms are too short to reach the really fattening stuff at the smorgasbord.

94. You're no longer part of the singles scene.

95. Garlic bread dipped in olive oil

96. She gets you.

97. It's your name she calls out when you have sex.

98. You bought Apple at seven.

99. A summer job at the beach

100. A reverse commute

101. While composing her honey-do list, your wife gets writer's block.

102. You have the acting chops to feign heartbreak when your in-laws announce they're cutting their stay short.

103. The protective spell that keeps your iPhone from being stolen

104. The Rapture turns out to be a Klondike Bar.

105. Your grandson is finally old enough to paint your fence.

106. The lump in your throat as you watch your little girl in the Christmas pageant

Miracle #6½:

The trooper nailed the guy behind you.

107. Water isn't fattening.

108. Dialing your ex after two bottles of Merlot and she's glad to hear from you

109. You know where your doc keeps the samples.

110. Your body mass index (BMI) responds favorably to Twizzlers.

111. The Snapple served in silver cocktail shakers at rehab

112. They have valet parking.

113. Your doctor would kill for your blood pressure.

114. Hitting the lottery four minutes after your divorce is finalized

115. The dreamy bicycle messenger asked you out.

116. You talked friends into allowing "miftxarpoop" as a Scrabble word.

117. You stepped barefoot on the *soft* Lego.

118. "Do I have someone for you!"

119. His DNA revealed no major character flaws.

120. You found your way out of Newark.

121. He opened the car door for you.

122. Learning from your mistakes so you can enjoy them when you make them again

Miracle #7:

The heroic 911 operator who calmly talked you through emptying a mouse trap.

123. Hearing your name called when you fly standby

124. Exploring scenic highways in a great car

125. "Next Rest Stop 33 Feet"

126. Twenty minutes at the blackjack table doubles your allowance.

127. Maui in January instead of Duluth

128. Your new dentures stand up even to mall food.

129.

That extra hour of sleep
when the clocks are
turned back

130. He knows how to use GPS to find your G-spot.

131. You're the teacher's pet (in the appropriate way).

132. Your cool dad buys cherry bombs instead of sparklers.

133. A glowing performance review

134. At last, you're the center of a scandal.

135. No more ramen—you finally made partner.

136. A contrite postal carrier who apologizes for delivering bills

Miracle #8:

An unexpected blizzard keeps everyone but you from the Prada sale.

137. They underestimated you.

138. Your name's on the guest list.

139. Your keys are right where you left them.

140. You sobbed your way out of a late fee.

141. When she tells you about her day, she goes for the abridged version.

142. He doesn't know he's funny but he makes you laugh.

143. Meat's back in style.

144. You know which is the fish fork.

145. Requited love

146. Gratitude

147. Drinking responsibly means leaving enough in the bottle for a nightcap.

148. Your own personal snowflake just landed on the tip of your nose.

149. Midnight Mass at Saint Patrick's Cathedral in New York City

150. A rented tux that fits like it's not rented

151. Getting off the subway just as the sax player jiggling a cup gets on

152. Returning the expensive dress you wore only once to a dinner party and not waking up in purgatory

153. Your new girlfriend's a pastry chef.

154.

Your husband's
too lazy to cheat.

155. Your immaculate taste

156. The smell of a new saddle

157. The smell of a new baseball glove

158. That perfect piña colada that allows you to be at one with nature

Miracle #9:

....

Every seat on your flight has too much legroom.

159. Redemption

160. Getting to choose which of the Ten Commandments apply to you

161. Saying what you really think gets you elected.

162. The scent of a just-peeled orange

163. You spot a gazebo just as a fierce summer shower begins.

164. Ants building an anthill—how do they know what to do?

165. You've been offered a lift to the Hamptons—via helicopter.

166. A spring night

167. A hayfield at dusk

168. That gorgeous reflection when you pass a shop window

169. Hearing your children laughing themselves sick

170. The levee held.

171. The waiter didn't follow you into the parking lot to ask, "How was everything?"

172. Friday afternoon finally came.

173. So did cocktail hour.

174. You are actually able to adjust your attitude.

175. Google's new "He's the Wrong Man for You" early warning detector

176. The perfect sports bra

177. Butter + salt + just-picked corn on the cob

178. Six hundred "winks" after Photoshopping whiter teeth on your profile

179.

She gained fifty
pounds after leaving you
for her trainer.

180.

With very few bruises,
you've mastered the art
of stopping on roller blades.

181. Slinky: the toy

182. Slinky: your hips

183. You ate saturated fat and didn't die.

184. The aroma when you open a new box of Crayolas

185. Burnt sienna

186. It's smudge-free.

Miracle #10:

You're blessed with that rare fifteen-year-old who doesn't know everything.

187. The brain-cleansing qualities of a major hit of wasabi

188. A gracious and leisurely lunch with your daughter home from college

189. Therapy's kicking in: You no longer cry at the sight of a bruised banana.

190. The mime ignored you.

191. You left Las Vegas with more than you came with.

192. She broke up with you on December 5— one less Christmas gift to buy.

193. Ella Fitzgerald singing anything

194. Whales frolicking

195.

Little girls deep in
conversation

196. The glory of a lightning storm

197. A Greyhound bus with an immaculate restroom

198. Nepotism

199. She's low maintenance.

200. Without hesitating, you immediately hand him a plane ticket when he announces, "I need my space."

201. The sweetness of an afternoon nap

202. You were reincarnated, this time with hair.

203. Baby's sonogram in high-def

204. A mild morphine drip gets you through the kitchen remodeling.

> ### Miracle #11:
> ....
> They finished on time.

205. And under budget.

206. Your high-priced escort showed up with a great assortment of dim sum and the financial pages.

207. Osteoporosis? At sixty-five, you have the bone density of a mastodon.

208.

The elevator actually *does* come faster when you press the button twenty-two times.

209. You weren't the last one chosen.

210. You've a remarkable talent for looking busy.

211. Burning incense in your cubicle helps you avoid unnecessary work.

212. Flash drives

213. You remembered to back it up.

214. "Daddy, watch me!"

215. He kept his word.

216. Feeling Dad's spirit when you put on his old biker jacket

217. Your belief is doubled when the prayer breakfast features blueberry pancakes.

218. A courageous student slipped a laxative into the school bully's Pepsi.

Miracle #12:
....

You don't have to sing, the bathroom lock works.

219. That scent of burning leaves on a fall day

220. Doing Venice with a gondolier who doesn't sing

221. It's not mold.

222. A bartender who fills your wineglass to the top

223. It's even better when reheated.

224. Your property taxes were lowered.

225. Closing your eyes and crossing your fingers really does prevent air turbulence.

226. Acceptance letters from your first-choice schools

227. The novel you wrote while living with your parents is short-listed for the Man Booker Prize ("Who knew?").

Miracle #12½:

Science develops a flu shot that also confers immunity to jerks.

---

228. There is no co-payment.

229. Your anxiety evaporated—he called off the wedding.

230. Clemency

231. Renewing your vows after twenty-five years of marriage

232. It wasn't malware.

233. Her quiet beauty

234. Spring in Appalachia

235. Autumn in Vermont

236. Being a lesbian means you never lament that all the good men are taken.

237. Your first grandchild

238. You're still able to walk after a pot roast brunch at Cracker Barrel.

239. Whitening strips

240. She gave you keys to her place (if only you had her address).

241. Great water pressure in the hotel shower

242. Even with hammertoes, the glass slipper fits.

243. You knew CPR.

244. A line around the block at the signing for your new book, *Healing by Getting Better*

245. You have the prostate of a teenager.

246. You successfully tunneled your way out of the nursing home.

247. Your new cardiologist wants you to eat more hot wings.

Miracle #13:

Claiming your tree house as a home office is cool with the IRS.

248. You have amazing parents.

249. Baby can't read but he changes his own diaper.

250. Your hidden talent for dancing like Gene Kelly after six Red Bulls

251. The homecoming float just ran over the guy who broke your heart.

252. Your chaperone for the junior prom has a tendency to nod off.

253. She has a thing for bald men.

254.

Pringles

255. Baby's little feet

256. The wine bar has a changing table.

257. An orchard

258. The wonderful man you're dating isn't fazed when you stop the car to administer last rites to roadkill.

259. Your knack for picking outfits means those extra fifteen pounds always contribute to that sought-after goddess look.

260. A toll bridge sign stating "Exact Change Only (Except You)"

261. Mob justice for the neighbor with a leaf blower

262. No backlash when you take the law into your own hands

263. Your stash of Moon Pies for when you run out of Paxil

264. You hide your anxieties well.

265. Birds flocking to your feeder for the Early Bird Special

266. "I'd like to thank the Academy . . ."

267. The dog really did eat your homework.

268. You saw something, you said something, and now you're on your honeymoon.

269. You still turn red and say, "Aw, shucks" when you shower with your wife of fifty years.

270. He doesn't know they're implants.

271. Spell-chek

272. A first date so terrific you don't notice how truly bad the restaurant's food is

273. Martha Stewart wants your personal input on her roast beef hash and her new hairdo.

274. She roared at your "You're not getting better, you're getting older" birthday card.

275. You're trapped in an elevator . . . with the guy delivering a pizza.

276. The soothing quality of a macaroni-and-cheese casserole

277. Your state's the first to recognize similar-sex marriage.

278. That adorable *plink-plink* sound of raindrops on your boyfriend's bald head

279. Lunesta

280. Hearing kitty purr is a can't-fail sleep aid.

281.

A comfortingly heavy picnic basket

282. John Philip Sousa's "The Stars and Stripes Forever"

283. He's also hopeless with chopsticks.

284. You thought you'd never get over him but you did.

285. Grandma's lemon ricotta cheesecake

286. Those few extra pounds make you look younger.

287. Grandma's minestrone

288. Grandma

289. The fjords of Norway

290. Escaping from a used-car lot alive

291. Your empathetic gynecologist prewarms the speculum.

292. Baby's eyes actually get bigger when he smiles.

293. They managed to get the stain out.

294. A five-hour flight and baby slept like a baby.

295. A little girl's bouncing pigtails

Miracle #14:
....
Your all-grown-up "little" daughter in her prom dress

296. The Golf Channel on a 50-inch Samsung

297. The fever broke.

298. That reassuring pile of warm, fluffy laundry

299. Your tech support's first language is English.

300. Successfully bluffing with a pair of threes

301. She can't recall what she was angry about.

302. She doesn't regard intimacy as a clear and present danger.

303. An onshore account your husband doesn't know about

304. You can drive a stick.

305. System Restore saved your life.

306. The car in front of you paid your toll.

307. Holding your life together with duct tape seems to be working.

308. You actually found romance on Craigslist, seven times.

309. With him you can wear heels.

310. He loves your smell.

311. WebMD confirms that you will live.

312. The bartender bought a round.

313. The mimosa matches your eyes (the Bloody Mary, not so much).

314. Washboard abs from lifting your feet when your husband vacuums

315. Elegance in all things

316. Deciding that the eleven pounds you gained on vacation are all muscle

317. Receiving a gift you didn't know you wanted

318. A cigar and fifty-year-old port with
     your son

319. She said "I love you" back.

320. They converted the tacky strip mall into a
     wildlife refuge.

321. The wine snob at your dinner party
     pronounces your $5.99 Syrah "lush,
     jammy, with just a hint of pepper,"
     then weeps when you tell him the price.

322. A summer share in a great beach house

323. Getting looped on rum and Coke

324. Gridlock and your bladder's empty

325. They delivered it when they said they
     would.

326. The "Mosquitoes Prohibited" sign on your
     hiking trail

327. Getting His undivided attention

328. Exquisite table manners get your meal comped

329. Happiness is a warm croissant.

330. Lighting that first candle as dusk settles

331. Noise-canceling headphones

332. Serenity

333. The warning label that just states "Be careful"

334. Her daughters think you're wonderful.

335. Legible subtitles

336. The peace when you listen to the third movement of Brahms's Third Symphony

337. W. C. Fields

338. Laurel and Hardy

339. The managing partner dressed as Wonder Woman on Casual Friday.

340. Your joke was tasteless but really funny.

341. Baby wipes that work just as well on non-babies

342. You passed your driving test.

343. Major Ugg shortage. Women are wearing flattering shoes again this winter!

344. Witness Protection relocated you near a Whole Foods.

Miracle #15:

....

Only three people on line at Trader Joe's

Miracle #16:

....

Your brother-in-law picked up a dinner check.

---

345. The slippers left behind by your previous boyfriend fit the new one.

346. The Surgeon General officially declares the bagel to be a portable version of chicken soup.

347. Walking to the tailor on a lovely spring day to have your slacks taken in

348.

Newly fallen snow that
keeps everything a secret

349. *A Christmas Carol* with Alastair Sim

350. Her scent on your pillow

351. Sunday morning with family

352. Our love

353. Authentic paella

354. Gentle overnight relief

355. Your grandfather fits in the shopping cart.

356. At Thanksgiving you're seated at the kiddie table—bless you, Botox.

357. Pandora Radio comes in loud and clear on your electronic ankle bracelet.

358. Nature obliged: A mane of blond hair that doesn't come from a bottle.

359. The waiter didn't introduce himself.

360. Fried anything

361. Raiding the fridge at 2 a.m. and finding treasure

362. You never expected to make this much money.

363. Going gray with elegance

364. You can tie a bow tie.

365. You know how to wear your jewelry as though there's plenty more at home.

366. Raves for your muscle tone from the officer who stops and frisks you

367. Your butcher has a crush on you.

368. Your first credit card

369. That first bite of a kick-ass spinach frittata

370. Unconditional love

371. Zappos

372. Zappos's return policy

373. The mall's lost-and-found helps you find your car.

374. A favorite aunt leaves you her secret recipe for chocolate chip cookies . . . and two acres of beachfront.

375. The person you kill over and over again in your thoughts just ate bad shrimp.

376. The hot health care aide has a thing for ancient men.

377. Your heart waited until after your daughter's wedding to have its attack.

378.

Blushing in the museum
when your lover kisses you
in front of Van Gogh's
Starry Night

379. Blushing outrageously when the guard cautions you for standing too close

380. The video of your herbal counselor scarfing down Milk Duds went viral.

381. Seals sunning themselves

382. Living on the one planet in our solar system with just the right amount of gravity

383. Your best friend is the only other person on the planet who doesn't know how to text.

384. A lunch-hour pedicure

385. Tuna sashimi

386. You created your own future.

387.

The hand-drawn
Mother's Day card from
your little ones

388. Sleeping late

389. It's cute that he thinks the squiggly arrow road sign means "Watch Out for Snakes."

390. Not a single raised eyebrow over your expense report

391. You didn't leave fingerprints.

392. No moldy strawberries at the bottom of the carton

393. It took just one pint of Grey Goose to break his vow of chastity.

394. Experian's gold star on your credit report

395. Your kids are perfect angels (sometimes).

396. Your blog, *Super-Amazing Me*, gets 50,000 daily hits.

397. The hard-to-see-but-definitely-there halos circling your children's little heads

398. A wild burst of inspiration produces your first-ever Creole knish.

399. "It's room service!"

400. Anything that overlooks Central Park

401. They didn't give up on you.

402. It ended up on someone else's tab.

Miracle #17:

....

Age spots magically vanish when a puppy licks your face.

403. Your dimples allow you to get away with anything.

404. Even in waders, your legs are luscious.

405. He thinks you're the bee's knees.

406. A hospital gown that closes all the way

407. You don't need back surgery.

408. The calorie-canceling effects of clasping your hands and saying a heartfelt grace before a heavy meal

409. It *does* taste like chicken.

410. Twins!

411. The sight of your beautiful wife nursing them

412. The picturesque little bed and breakfast where the owners stay out of sight for the entire weekend

413. Enough ice

414. Parents who bankroll your acting career

415. Bar Mitzvah loot

416. The stuff from your parents' summer house goes well in your dorm room.

417. Finding an original Honus Wagner baseball card in your grandfather's Bible

418. At sixty, your boobs are still defying gravity.

419. Your second honeymoon is even better than the first, and with the same spouse.

420. A suite at the Waldorf, just because

421. She left a toothbrush.

422.

Finding your happy
place with a mojito that's
loaded with vitamins

423. It was insured.

424. Healthy decadence: ice cream and cold pizza for breakfast

425. Your mistress isn't litigious.

426. "Sir, your table is ready."

427. There is no paper trail.

428. Your home's drywall was not made in China.

429. Stamping your foot really did make the bus come faster.

430. Heel spurs that go away because you make them feel unwanted

431. Cookie jars

432.

Porcelain teapots

433. A real Yule log on the Christmas fire

434. You recycle.

435. Nothing happened when you changed lanes without signaling.

Miracle #18:

You're both still more sexually active than your twenty-five-year-old.

436. Jussi Björling singing "O Holy Night"

437. The Song of Solomon

438. Any physical exam where you needn't remove your underwear

439. Former high school students coming back to thank you (and several finally turning in their past-due homework assignments)

440. He actually noticed that you got your hair cut.

441. All 2,000 of your Facebook friends show up with chicken soup when you're sick.

442. Size didn't matter.

443. He didn't choke when you uttered the word, "commitment."

444.

Passing the Statue of
Liberty as you sail into
New York harbor

445. A loving husband who understands the real meaning of "I'll just be a minute"

446. Regularity

447. A mysterious stranger pays it forward by shoveling your driveway.

448. The oddly refreshing hallucinatory effects of Aunt Martha's baba au rhum

449. You and your wife forgot what you were fighting about.

450. Make-up sex

451. With your cholesterol you need not consider butter a dirty word.

452. The app that straightens your closet

453.

The amazing social
possibilities when
you hitchhike in your
Harley jacket

454. Snuggling with a cute guy under a blanket at the homecoming game, and you don't even know his name

455. The YouTube clip of you jitterbugging in stilts has gone viral.

456. Finding a Starbucks in the rain forest

457. He got up at 3 a.m. to bail you out.

458. The sun breaking through the clouds at just the right moment

459. She looks even more amazing with her clothes off.

460.

You found the spot
where the squirrel is
entering the house.

461. Hearing "I've got it under control, Dad," when you decide to tell your son about the birds and the bees

462. Spotting the Dalai Lama at anger management class

463. You saw it coming.

464. Your little one's gifted, and coordinated.

465. Your AA sponsor is someone famous.

466. One day at a time is working.

Miracle #19:

....

Ikea's furniture now assembles itself.

467. Eating lobster with forceps

468. Passing an afternoon rereading your husband's first romantic e-mails

469. Someone, somewhere, isn't writing a memoir.

470. Someone, somewhere, isn't writing a book about Marilyn Monroe.

471. "Press one to speak to someone smart."

472. Graceland on weed

473. A "brilliant idea" that changes your life

474. Ralph Lauren's new spring hazmat outfit

475.

High cheekbones

476. Three pregnancies and no stretch marks

477. The instant antidepressive effects of a black-and-white cookie

478. A transformative experience

479. Your nutritionist called in sick—he ate too many herbs.

480. Thunder and lightning to remind you of the wonder of it all

481. The Painted Desert at sunrise

482. Having children who change you for the better

483. A great dinner party with great guests

484. It's only a flesh wound.

485. A work-optional Casual Friday

486. The generous decorating allowance for your new corner office

487. Only four days of mild depression when you see your new passport photo

488. Popping bubble wrap while your wife asks, "Are you listening to me?"

489. You both sneaked an entire pizza into the movie theater.

490. Your MacArthur "genius grant"

491. The Founding Fathers

Miracle #20:

The glory of our Constitution

---

492. A bidding war for your house

493. Avoiding a traffic ticket by wiggling your ears

494. Workers' comp for the paper cut

495. Snuggling into thick flannel pajamas from L. L. Bean

496. The secret language between you and your twin

497. "Sir, you forgot your change."

498. She likes her steak rare.

499. He melts when you cry.

500. She doesn't want alimony.

501. Minimal pouting from Mr. Gino when you change hairdressers

502. The bangs are reversible.

503. Someday pleated slacks will be back.

504. An Elvis sighting in your compost pile

505. The client loves it.

506. Feeling baby's reassuring kicks

507. Your little boy passes gas that combines the scent of the sea with patchouli.

508. The flight you just missed has been sitting on the tarmac for five hours.

509. You weren't the first to arrive.

510. Fresh powder

511. You weren't spotted sneaking off to the bunny hill at the ski slope.

512. It's only a scratch.

513. The dial on your bathroom scale reads "Good news!"

514. While salvaging a crumbling barn, you find Iggy Pop under the floorboards.

515. Climbing the Alps in a Vespa

516. You find a warm waffle tucked into your JetBlue seat-back pocket.

517. Freckles are back in style.

518. Air-conditioning

519. You unclogged the sink yourself.

520. They didn't check your references.

521. Panicking as you approach a sobriety checkpoint until you realize you're in a cab

522. Post-golf whiskey sours at the club

523. Needing a bladder break every seventy-two miles makes him love you even more.

524. Good advice

525. It's never too late.

526. The happy ending when you skip the war part of *War and Peace*

527. Wearing heels all day that don't hurt

528. Oozing sexiness when you wear your Calypso flip-flops

529. You won her over with your chicken sausage gumbo (spicy, but not too).

530. She's clingy only when she helps you stumble home after six gin and tonics.

531. 78,000 views of your YouTube video of him begging you to take him back

532. They're chocolate sprinkles, not mouse droppings.

533. "Made in America"

534. Finally leaving your comfort zone and discovering bliss

535. You caught the bouquet.

536. She had jumper cables.

537. Spooning with the one you love

538. Your wonderfully crazy kids

539. A good mind and the cleft in your chin get you a Fulbright.

540. The Golden Gate Bridge at dawn

541. A private jet to the Super Bowl

542. A car-horn-free Manhattan

543. Those memories of a blistering summer romance with a ranch hand that are getting you through menopause

544. He still thinks of you.

545. Tucking in your three-year-old after he reads you a bedtime story

546. Hot chocolate made right

547. Our Earth is at the perfect distance from the Sun.

548. Heroes (the brave)

549. Heroes (the sandwich)

550. Feeling instantly peaceful when you light a votive candle

551. He knows where to touch you.

552. They're blown away by the supreme flakiness of your pie crust.

553. A gorgeous, healthy baby and (little bonus) no hemorrhoids for Mommy

554. It's rent controlled.

555. A week-long happy hour

556. Maternity leave in the South of France

557. The support tech actually helped.

Miracle #21:

Your wild teenage daughter wants to spend spring break with the Amish.

---

558. Putting on warm jeans straight from the dryer

559. You love thy neighbor (she doesn't pull the shades).

560. Doing Jell-O shots with your cool probation officer

561. Seats behind home plate

562. Finally finding a bathing suit that hides your secrets

563. You're being stalked by an A-list celebrity.

564. Breath mints

565. Your ex-husband's leggy new girlfriend has spider veins.

566. The mystery of genius

567. An honest plumber ("It just needs a washer.")

568. You've mastered the metric system.

569. Painters who leave your place spotless

570. Your coworker somehow forgot to show you the twenty-six photos of her cat playing chess.

571. Surviving a boring dinner party by polishing the host's silver

572. You got the good friends when your marriage ended.

573. That fabulous Louboutin bag gets you priority boarding.

574. Your four-year-old in your heels

575. A next-day meatloaf sandwich

576. Coed dorms

577. Your daughter dropped out of film school to become a surgeon.

578. Combining tailgating with the commencement speech

579. A root beer float on a sweltering day served in a frosty mug

580. Whistles from construction workers and you just turned seventy

581. Your belief in Creationism (that extraordinary gift of being able to create a credible lie when calling in sick)

582. Evolution

583. Your stockpile of empty Tiffany boxes

584. Your uncanny ability to undetectably re-gift gifts

585. Goodbye, dreadful candy dish

586. Your wholesome teenager still thinks that S&M is a supermarket.

587. Rising to sing the "Hallelujah Chorus"

588. When you run back frantic to the public lavatory, your Rolex is right where you left it on the sink.

589. You never took Madoff's calls.

590. You got into Princeton on your own.

591. Your new eye shadow morphs you from mousy Republican to independent femme fatale.

592. Charlie Rose actually let you answer a question.

593. Looking really great in the dress you lost ten pounds for

594. He came crawling back.

595. Your knees are still unacquainted with cortisone.

596.

The check cleared.

597. He doesn't get all grumpy when you go antiquing.

598. You died with all of your teeth.

599. Hitting "Delete" on a Christmas letter that begins "It's been a year of reflection, growth and some really downer stuff . . ."

600. The arrogant Burger King supervisor who downsized you is now taking your order.

601. You got out moments before the bubble burst.

602. It's not your ankle in the bungee cord.

603. Knee socks that stay up

604. Your kids still think that Lincoln Logs are high-tech.

605. Spending your vacation ice fishing in Key West

606. He quit before you had to endure the agony of firing him.

607. Finding the love that changes your life

608. Traveling on the Venice Simplon-Orient-Express

609. Using a carrier pigeon instead of tweeting (it's more romantic)

610. Eating at a place called "Mom's" and not getting sick

611. The agony of having several top preschools fighting for your kid

Miracle #22:

Finding a crumpled twenty in the jeans you haven't worn for ages

612. Sailing off to dreamland on 600-thread-count Egyptian cotton sheets

613. Waking up next to the one you love

614. The slinky black dress you had to be pushed into did exactly what it was supposed to do.

615. The snoring in the jury box isn't coming from you.

616. Her roommate's gone for the weekend.

617.

They deliver.

618. Mailing the last car payment

619. "Paid in full."

620. He also likes pretzels dipped in Nutella.

621. Peanut butter, too.

Miracle #23:

....

While digging around in the dairy case for milk with the latest expiration date, you find a watch.

---

622. It came up "0.0" on the Breathalyzer.

623. Your integrity

624. Shedding the right kind of tears

625. Your new tattoo is the talk of the oil rig.

626. Earthy women

627. Unpretentious men

628. Being good to yourself

629. OD'ing on pecan sandies

630. A friend who tells you the truth

631. "Honey, I'm home."

632. They still can't hit your fastball.

Miracle #24:
....

Your wedding announcement made The
New York Times.

633. An arranged marriage that turns out great

634. A powerful self-esteem that isn't damaged when the person handing out flyers doesn't give you one

635. Burglars stole the Christmas ham but overlooked your jewelry.

636. You drink before noon only when your mother calls.

637. Catching a home-run ball at the World Series

638. A secret smile because you look healthier than the other patients in your doctor's waiting room

639. A happy ending from the TSA screener

640. The hitchhiking scene in It Happened One Night

641. You were wearing clean underwear when the car hit you.

642. You're blessed with optimism—you see your bladder as half full.

643. Your little girl's eyes when she shakes a snow globe

644. Training wheels

645. Line-dried sheets

646. The day you shed your training wheels

647. Closing on your first house

648. Your know-it-all life coach is living in his car.

649. Just when you need one, an expert on Byzantine Greek hagiographical manuscripts shows up.

650. Watching your daughter graduate from medical school

651. Yours is the sweetest breath at the party.

652. They caught it early.

653. Your stellar buffalo-wing-eating talents

654. Your diary is password protected.

655. Those holiday visions of sugarplums after three of Uncle Benny's eggnogs

656. Double karma points when you take the shoes that pinch so you don't hurt the salesman's feelings

657. Finding another car when you clean out the garage

658. You just sent the IRS a check for $346,766. Life is good—buy a bigger private jet.

659. Chopin, Champagne and tea lights

660. Power-eating Tostitos

661. You prayed away your belly fat.

662. And your muffin top.

663. Those chocolate malted-milk balls in your dentist's goody bag (to boost your immune system)

664. Sunlight filtering through a spiderweb

665. A lint roller when you need one

666. The dent doesn't show.

667. Using your new Dyson to vacuum up the ashes of a dead relationship

668.

You still ski with your
original hips.

669. You successfully hid behind the sofa when your ne'er-do-well cousins rang your bell.

670. She let you put your arm around her.

671. That first sight of your beautiful and perfect wedding cake

672. Extending your pinky and sneaking a tiny taste of the frosting

673. Finding a little lost penguin while cleaning out your freezer

674. A super-terrific neighbor who lends you her husband so you can use the HOV lane

675. He passes your first-date litmus test (he's not wearing tube socks).

676. Sneaking a kiss in a Gap dressing room

677. Three months without a cigarette and you've lost twelve pounds

678. "You never seem to age!"

679. The pyramids

680. An emergency chute

681. A pain-free catheter

682. The first time you make love to the person you love

683. It's your lipstick on his collar.

684. Being a fly on the wall of your little girl's first tea party

685. Getting the okay from your accountant to toss eleven cartons and twenty-two years' worth of receipts

686. You had the courage to say no to an aggressive telemarketer and a controlling mother on the same day.

687. Your forty-seven-year-old son finally left home.

688. Customs merely smiled at the cheese, wine, sausage, bread, corkscrew, knife and hotel towels in your carry-on.

689. Riding through your old neighborhood in a limo

690. "May I have your autograph?"

Miracle #25:

Your cool new personal trainer lets you count rising from the toilet as a sit-up.

691. Instead of violent video games, your son prefers the minor Elizabethan poets.

692. A mere three months since the breakup and you can hear "our song" on the car radio without driving into a guardrail.

693. Closing your eyes and freebasing lemon meringue tarts when you reach your weight-loss goal

694. One try blows out all ninety candles on your birthday cake.

695. You know how to use the word "louche" in a conversation.

696. Your legs look great, even in Crocs.

697.

You're blessed with great
dental insurance.

698. "Jet skis prohibited under penalty of death."

699. An early-morning glide over a silent lake in a kayak

700. House-sitting in Bermuda

701. It's a dust ball, not a mouse.

702. It's all water weight.

703. Leaving the restaurant on a freezing night and discovering that coat check gave you back a warmer coat

704. Her voice tells you that she's glad you called.

705. Everyone in the world has split ends except you.

706. Open house at your little boy's play fort

707. You're starting at the top.

708. Your first paycheck

709. You found the one empty parking space in Manhattan.

710. They opened the wine that *you* brought to the White House dinner.

711. The manager cheerfully accepted your reason for returning the garment. ("It did nothing for my social life.")

712. You listened to your gut.

713. Mood swings that only go from high to higher

714.

Xanax

715. Using your finger instead of a swizzle stick to stir your cocktail enchants her (she goes for quirky).

716. Your enviable golf swing

717. Favorable publicity

Miracle #26:
....

A nooner with your wife while the kids are at school

718. Assisted living means a barstool with arms.

719. A loving trophy wife who cuts your meat

720. Talking your parents out of putting on Chubby Checker and doing the twist at your sweet sixteen party

721. They allow you to hang your Yale diploma in your toll booth.

722. Converting your carbon credits into air miles

723. The deer hate your hedges.

724. Dozing off on the patio on a bug-free morning

725. Watching your parents waltz at their fiftieth wedding anniversary

726. The Great Lakes

727. The smell of a new Bible

728. A TV deal for your blog on the food served at wakes

729. Dickens, a wing chair and white wine on a rainy day

730. Giving up celery and losing three pounds

731. You forgot your password but remember your first dog's name.

732. Your new medication has some really cool side effects.

733. Texting your confession to a techie priest

734. Eating a chocolate chip cookie while it's still hot and melty

735. Your dark past—and she wants to hear about it

736. You're cool with being shallow.

737. Finding deliverance in a stack of old-fashioned sour cream waffles with butter and maple syrup

738. Getting through the sermon by sipping Jack Daniels through a straw

739. You got a producing credit.

740. A triathlon whose events include distance running, swimming and speed-eating Tuscan white bean soup and chicken Milanese (with arugula)

741. The off-label use of a knish gives you stamina to read *Moby Dick*.

742. Needing both hands to count your blessings

743. You're going to need a wealth management team.

744. Tenure

745. She prefers a pub to a tearoom.

746. Locked out—but the spare key is where you hid it

747. Baby polar bears

748. Monopoly—and you own all the good properties

749. Christmas windows

750. Animal shelters

751. A thoughtful soul finally chokes the bird in the cuckoo clock.

752. While you're attempting to merge, the guy in the other car smiles and waves you in.

753. Lifting your little one above your head so she can place the star atop the Christmas tree.

754. God-fearing atheists

755. Your car runs on coffee.

756. It wasn't a dream.

757. Your parents didn't name you Apple.

758. You've never had a migraine.

759. An invitation to the fabulous party

760. Getting wasted on tiramisu when you pass the bar exam

761. You pulled the cat from the dryer before Mom got home.

762. An honorary degree from the same university where security once escorted you off the campus

763. An outside stateroom

764. Boarding the cruise ship with a waterproof watch (you never know)

765. You don't look totally weird in cruisewear.

766. Your sweetheart left her husband and needs a place to stay.

767. She looks even better in a bathing suit.

768. They can't start the meeting without you.

769. A pleasant surprise when you open your year-end bonus

770. Your fruitcake-doorstop is a hit with your in-laws.

771. Wearing white to a wine tasting and leaving unstained

772. Applause from other restaurant patrons when you deck a condescending French waiter for correcting your pronunciation

773. A double helping of four-berry pie with nut/crumble topping because your pants are baggy

774. Passing the exhaust fan of a bakery while they're baking bread

775. Your charisma

776. No regrets

> ### Miracle #27:
> ....
>
> The moratorium on TV has the family talking to one another.

777. You were picked first.

778. He's thrilled that your mother is moving in.

779. Dish TV in the Hereafter

780. A friendship bracelet from your little niece

781. Golden Lab puppies

782. Your ex took the kids for the weekend— hello, unlimited golf.

783. Jacuzzi, here we come.

784. Your back-up villa in the South of France should your neighbors in the Hamptons be hateful

785. The dreaded whine gene skipped your kids.

786. Passing your driver's test on the first try

787. A pedicure at your desk, boss's treat

788. The Nutritional Food Pyramid includes farm-fresh Pop Tarts.

789. You wished upon the correct star.

790. Your seven-year-old playing Ophelia in her school's production of *Hamlet*

791. The stroller bearing down on you swerved at the last minute.

792. You funded your root canal with a bake sale.

793. Angst over which of the three job offers to accept

794. A secure retirement

795. Greta Garbo in *Ninotchka*

796. The Amalfi coast in an Alfa Romeo

797. A real sleigh ride with bells, snow, horses and loved ones

798. Switching to brown rice only really does get rid of cellulite.

799. Ducks shepherding their little ducklings

800. A surprise visit from a butterfly

801. Your hairdresser charges extra because your hair is so thick.

802. Your weekend guest knows how to put up drywall.

803. A bed pre-pre-warmed by two dogs and three cats

804. You lied about your age but he lied about his height.

805. Celebrating your formal induction into the exclusive "We Don't Own a Cell Phone" club (dues-paying membership: eight people)

806. While nattering on about himself, your blind date swallows the little parasol in his mai tai.

Miracle #28:

Today you have the Grand Canyon all to yourself.

807. The naughty schoolgirl outfit worn by your dental hygienist

808. The bark of a rescue dog

809. Your first time on snowshoes

810. For Lent, he's giving up bay rum.

811. She can hang a picture.

812. The dimly lit restaurant prints their menus in 20-point type:

Bayou Butter Crawfish $24.95

813. You're still on the good side of thirty.

814.

You have the knees
for a kilt.

815. You have the thighs for tennis.

816. You see the irony but not the conflict between "passion for life" and "couch potato."

817. She takes off her earrings to dance.

818. Rubbing your cheek with cherry strudel somehow eliminates morning sickness.

819. The toddler sitting behind you on the plane is too short to kick your seat.

820. Bach

821. Billie Holiday

822. The flawless *poutine* in Quebec

823. You look good in anything.[1]

824. Feng-shui-ing the vegetables in your fridge keeps them fresh longer.

---

[1] Except Birkenstocks.

825.

Your upper arms can still handle a sleeveless dress.

> ### Miracle #29:
> ....
>
> Swearing at the hinge made it stop squeaking.

826. The critics were wrong.

827. The passion-arousing possibilities of a warm prune Danish

828. You made him blush.

829. He's in the mood.

830. It's only fractured, not broken.

831. Cataracts prevent your mother-in-law from seeing the dust bunnies.

832. The IRS agent begins the audit by pulling out a bottle of single malt.

833. A bottom-of-the-purse stash of emergency tampons

834. Being strong and saying no to buying the extended warranty

835. Your baby's a cheap laugh.

Miracle #30:
....

Three children, a peanut butter addiction, and still no "mom butt"

836.

The right people RSVP'd.

837. The cad who dumped you via text message fell off a roller coaster.

838. The co-op board loves you! ☺ ☺ ☺ ☺

839. Yes, you are worthy.

840. You got a radar detector for Chanukah.

> ## Miracle #31:
>
> Ketchup

Miracle #32:

....

Ketchup on everything

841. Your secret passion

842. Waffle cones

843. The water slides in Heaven

844. A killer tan that makes everyone in the room hate you

845. A teddy bear to whom you can tell everything

846. The plane didn't run out of runway.

847. The paparazzi have no idea it's you.

848. A buffet so lavish you must be hosed down
between courses

849. Honey mustard

850. WD-40

851. Red Wing boots

852. Enhancing the healthful effects of herbal
tea with tequila

853. You taught your cat to fetch your slippers.

854. Trading sex for Invisaligns

855. That sense of well-being when your
daughter calls when she said she would

856. The causal connection between male
virility and Cheetos

857. A full-size spare in the trunk

858. The glimpse of cleavage when your fairy
godmother bends over

859. You can say "Where's a bathroom?" in nine languages.

860. A rainy-day Three Stooges marathon with a skid of potato chips and a twelve-pack

861. Discovering an Oreo in the sofa

862. The wellness center serves lean pastrami.

863. He shaves your legs better than you do.

864. NASA's invention of the nonskid toupee

865. Sitting around the campfire with friends, and you're the one with the marshmallows

866. This time your son called for advice, not a loan.

867. Your children finally admit that their parents weren't the problem.

868. An arsenal of daydreams

869. You no longer need to order the cheapest thing on the menu.

870. Flying over America on a cloudless day

871. Hello, ecstasy! There's your luggage on the carousel.

872. Vanilla ice cream with flecks of vanilla bean

873. No guilt when reading a trashy novel on the beach

874. No guilt when you watch reality TV

875. For Christmas, your usually practical aunt gave you a Louis Vuitton instead of a loom.

876. The trooper lets you off with just a warning, and her phone number.

877. Your ability to explain the difference between hollandaise sauce and béchamel impresses the hell out of her.

878. Reassuring "Don't worry about me" tweets from your cat when you're at work

879. A parrot who knows when to keep his beak shut

880. Pitiful whimpering gets your allowance raised.

881. It takes just one grenade to silence the wailing car alarm.

882. Your karaoke rendition of "Who Let the Dogs Out" didn't *totally* clear the room.

883. Your body *is* a temple.

884. Speed-dating on weed

885. Visine

886. You're up to the responsibilities of being the Center of the Universe.

887. It's love, not vertigo.

888. Forgiveness

889. Leaving a Walmart "door-buster" sale with all your teeth

890. A devoted wife who lets you sleep undisturbed through five hours of Wagner

891. Waking up in the morning and touching your wife

892. Watching the game from your boss's skybox

893. Louis Armstrong

894. Mozart's clarinet quintet

895. Your holistic health guru has no problem using "wellness" and "Reese's Peanut Butter Cups" in the same sentence.

896. It took just three marriages to finally find a husband who doesn't snore.

897. A cat with low expectations

898. Your unshakable faith in your faith

> ### Miracle #33:
> ....
> Your diet's coming true!

899. No spanking from Weight Watchers when you test positive for cherry pie à la mode

900. Your ability to steer the conversation back to your triple bypass

901. Being marooned on a desert isle with a supermodel who knows several ways to cook fish

902. The pride in your "My Son Is Performing Community Service" bumper sticker

903. Jumper cables

904. Aspirin

905. A dive bar that leaves its Christmas decorations up forever

906. The afterlife turns out better than this one.

907. It rained *after* the picnic.

908. Hacking your lover's e-mail confirms that she loves only you.

Miracle #34:

Hanging a Saint Christopher medal from your rearview mirror earns a rate reduction from Geico.

Miracle #35:

....

An '82 Margaux and a straw in your Christmas stocking

909. The nice judge lets you work off unpaid parking tickets by modeling his closetful of Jimmy Choos.

910. Beating your brothers to the last vanilla icing cupcake

911. They don't suspect that your jewelry's rented.

912. The herb garden on your windowsill

913. You've buried two oncologists.

Miracle #36:

It's a takeout menu under the door, not a subpoena.

914. Horses

915. Disney World on Ecstasy

916. The hotel mini-bar comes with hash browns.

917. Caller ID

918. She sent over a drink.

919. Raccoons respect your "No Trespassing" sign.

920. Wedding toasts that make you teary

921. Your voice finally changed.

922. Your financial adviser showed you ten terrific ways to spend your windfall.

923. The transformative power of a Savile Row suit

924. A promotion for presenting the annual report in iambic pentameter

925. A controlled experiment that involves
eating all the chocolate truffles you want

926. The Ghent Altarpiece

927. Antilock brakes

928. The thousands of calories burned when you
reorganize your closet

929. "When can you start?"

930. The love of your life in a diaphanous
summer frock

931. You got out of the mosh pit alive
(but you're wearing someone else's
shoes).

932. Santa took care of your student loan debt.

933. A smile that gets you bumped to first class

Miracle #37:
....

An okay from your doc to start smoking
until you get over her

---

934. Your post-holiday paunch is actually an optical illusion.

935. You stopped singing before the elevator doors opened.

936. You're not the one stripping wallpaper.

937. "Hello, you have six messages, all of them terrific."

938. At eighty-five, you're still strong enough to pull your dog in a direction he doesn't want to go.

939. Your parents let you swap Little League for bassoon lessons.

940. No strollers parked in front of your favorite dive bar

941. *He* gave us opposable thumbs so we can text.

942. Flawless cottage fries with just the hint of sea salt

Miracle #38:

....

An eligible bachelor joined your book club.

943.

You have the toes
for sandals.

Miracle #39:

....

A perfect parallel park on the first try

944. A dollar for a mint Gene Autry lunchbox at a yard sale

945. Finally giving in to temptation makes you bloom.

946. You'll need a bigger safety deposit box— your wealthy aunt passed away.

947. Your neighbor finally returned the drill he borrowed 3.2 years ago.

948. Eat-in kitchens

949.

A hawk flew off with your
neighbor's wind chimes.

950. Nobody knows about your secret life as a furniture salesman.

951. Your shrink assures you that alphabetizing your psych meds at 4:20 a.m. is normal and healthy.

952. Decluttering your apartment reveals a window you didn't know was there.

953. The babysitting gig has a pension plan.

954. Your culinary skills include speed-chopping vegetables with no sign of blood.

Miracle #40:

You were smart enough to choose the right parents.

955. The summit of Pikes Peak with a Cuban cigar and a snifter of single malt

956. That abundant flow of saliva as the waitress approaches with your hot fudge sundae

957. "So, where do you work out?"

958. "Have you been working out?" (acceptable variation)

959. Yet another Michelin star for your kids' lemonade stand

960. You discovered a new way to torture your little brother.

961.

Unwinding at the end of
the day with your
wonderful wife's
medical-grade martinis

962. Your cat doesn't sleep around.

963. Your first public appearance while wearing your new engagement ring

964. Your Led Zeppelin T-shirt survived yet another washing.

965. The carriage house comes with it.

966.

"Batteries included."

967. You know where the bodies are buried.

968. You managed to peel the uncanceled stamp off the envelope.

Miracle #41:

You got a callback.

969.

On Christmas morning,
your nephew plays only
with your gift.

970. Mortgage rates have hit an all-time low.

971. A cherry blossom festival without allergies

972. The profound lack of interest in your home displayed by termites

973. You're out of danger.

974. That delicious end-of-day moment when you slip out of Blahniks and into old frayed Keds

---

Miracle #42:
....

You're eight and a half months pregnant and he thinks your waddle is extra-sexy.

---

975. No charge to replace the broken crown. Dentist insists that it's "my bad" that he didn't warn you about Gummy Bears.

976. Slowly sinking into a glass of chilled Chardonnay and a hot bath

Miracle #43:

Those secret orgasms in yoga class

977. It only takes you ten minutes to deal well with your feelings of abandonment when no one important calls for ten minutes.

978. A corny anniversary card from hubby

979. Social Security is there for you.

980. Rebooting worked.

981. That light at the end of the tunnel means your colonoscopy's done.

982. A cup holder on your new hard drive

983. CliffsNotes

984. Salvation

985. Your pilot has gray hair.

986. Identity crisis over—you no longer think you're Beowulf.

987. It's him on your voicemail.

Miracle #44:

You arrived too late to catch the ventriloquist.

988. Pilfering candy from your kids' Halloween stash and not getting caught

989. Looking innocent when confronted

990. You don't hate yourself in the morning.

991. Smiling at the office gossip when you wear the same outfit today that you wore yesterday

992. An office romance that blossoms into a killer severance package

Miracle #45:

Sending in the last mortgage payment

993. Falling to your knees makes God feel needed.

994. A heated pew

995. Redwood trees

996. A glorious sunset

> ### Miracle #46:
> ....
> Seeing the doctor at 10:47 when you have a 10:45 appointment

997. The push-up bra

998. Beethoven

999. It came out just like the cookbook swore it
would.

1000. The mysteries that are best left unsolved

1001. Death by cake

Tarcher's delightfully disgusting miscellany series

A fascinating yet oddball catalogue of facts about the human body

A *New York Times* bestseller*

978-1-58542-645-4

$12.95

A complete guide to everything bizarre and, at times, nauseating under the sun

978-1-58542-757-4

$12.95

A universe of minutiae that one may want to know (and a few things one may not) about the animal kingdom

978-1-58542-799-4

$12.95

*extended list